On the Line

To STephe,
with best wishes
& Thanks for your work!
from Gardner
5.19.19

poems by

Gardner McFall

Finishing Line Press
Georgetown, Kentucky

On the Line

ACKNOWLEDGMENTS

I am grateful to the editors of the following magazine where these poems
first appeared:

The Agni Review: "The Pilot's Daughter"
Crazyhorse: "The Air Pilot's Wife"
The Missouri Review: "Blue Raft," "Four Corners," and "Missing"
The Nation: "Moves"
The New Republic: "Ornaments in August"
Pequod: "Mission in Hong Kong"
Ploughshares: "Facts"
Poet Lore: "My Father Meets Amelia Earhart," "Stopping at the True, the
    Good, the Beautiful Company in Bac Ninh," and "Veterans Day"
River Styx: "Water Buffalo"
The Sewanee Review: "Leonidas at Thermopylae"

"Blue Raft," "Missing," and "On the Line" are included in *Inheriting the War:
Poetry and Prose by Descendants of Vietnam Veterans and Refugees,* edited
by Laren McClung with a Foreword by Yusef Komunyakaa (Norton, 2018);
I am grateful to the Corporation of Yaddo, the MacDowell Colony, and the
Virginia Center for the Creative Arts for their support over the years.

Publisher: Leah Maines
Editor: Christen Kincaid
Cover Art: Cdr. A. Dodge McFall's 1965 targeting map,
        Photo by Gardner McFall
Author Photo: Susan Unterberg
Cover Design: Leah Maines

Printed in the USA on acid-free paper.
Order online: www.finishinglinepress.com
        also available on amazon.com

Author inquiries and mail orders:
Finishing Line Press
P. O. Box 1626
Georgetown, Kentucky 40324
U. S. A.

Table of Contents

In memory of my father and mother
& for my dearest Peter, Amanda, Dodge

Four Corners

Two parents in front, two children in back,
driving west in the hottest part of summer.
The dog's ears flapped in the wind.
Nothing could relieve that heat, not even

the soft drinks fished from our ice-chest.
In Kansas we counted the silos and fields;
then, after the Rockies, all the trading posts,
whose outdoor curios and blanket displays

gathered dust from the speeding trucks.
Late afternoon, our interest in scenery
fell on the possibility of a motel pool.
That's when we happened to spot the sign,

Four Corners. We found it described
in Fodor's Guide: marked by a low, square
monument, the state lines of Arizona, Utah,
Colorado, and New Mexico, meeting in the middle.

It could have been anywhere if you believe
what you read. Hardly anything distinguished
that point where four states touch,
but we stopped the car. A man took our picture

to prove we were there, balanced together
on a concrete slab small as a kitchen table,
shoulder to shoulder, each in a different state,
our hair blowing in the same direction.

Moves

When the movers leave my mother's china
and linen in the rain in the front yard
of the penultimate place we're stationed,
she sits down among the boxes
scattered like a child's blocks
and says, I'm never moving again.
She's almost right.
There's only one more move, out to Lemoore,
where VA-76 will leave for Vietnam.
And when she gets there,
she wants to go home, suddenly,
where her family is.
So my father drives us eighty miles an hour
cross-country and flies back
to take the squadron on a second tour.
Though he's gone, though he's been gone
more years than he's been at home,
we carry on our ordinary lives.
I wear a sky-dyed uniform each day
to the local school for girls;
my brother joins Cub Scouts.
Mother volunteers at Navy Relief.
When the glossy military car pulls up,
my mother is not home,
not sitting down collected,
but driving up the street
with bags of groceries in the back seat.
And even when she sees it,
she thinks nothing of it.
She thinks it's a social call.
Only when the chaplain gets out
does the thought cross her mind.

Then, she begins to shake.
Grief travels toward you this way
out of the blue. It finds you
unprepared, as when you spy
your mother across the asphalt
basketball court where she's come
to retrieve you from school,
and she puts her arm around you
somewhere between gym and world history
and says, your father is missing.

Missing

For years I lived with the thought
of his return. I imagined he had ditched
the plane and was living on a distant
island, plotting his way back
with a faithful guide; or, if
he didn't have a guide, he was sending
up a flare in sight of an approaching ship.

Perhaps having reached an Asian capital
he was buying gifts for a reunion
that would dwarf the ones before.
He would have exotic stories to tell,
though after a while, the stories
didn't matter or the gifts.

One day I told myself, he is not coming
home, though I had no evidence,
no grave, nothing to say a prayer over.
I knew he was flying among the starry
plankton, detained forever.
But telling myself this was as futile
as when I found a picture of him

sleeping in the ready room,
hands folded across his chest,
exhausted from the sortie he'd flown.
His flight suit was still on,
a jacket collapsed at his feet.
I half thought I could reach out

and wake him, as the unconscious
touches the object of its desire
and makes it live. I have kept
all the doors open in my life
so that he could walk in, unsure
as I've been how to relinquish
what is not there.

On the Line

The line where you were,
like the equator, divided the world
in two. Whatever the latitude,
the planes roared off the carrier.
Their bombs fell vertically
on target. In a letter you wrote,

"Each day we bomb the Ho Chi Minh Trail,
they reconstruct it by night.
We can't win, but don't quote me."
You were a kind man.
You loved your family.
For years I've tried to figure

what you loved more—
not the military life with tours of duty
or the jungle war. You loved
Duty itself, a word, an abstraction.
Now our lines of communication
are cut, except for your blood in me.

These words, strange as your death,
fall as on foreign villages,
unpronounceable names,
all lost on American ears.
I am traveling fast, propelled
by you, doing what I must,
ready to answer for it.

Facts

In your orange flight suit, you approached the Renault
we knew might stall after a hard winter freeze.
With your pilot's hand, you turned the engine.
When it caught, I ran down the walkway you'd shoveled.

Cinderella lunchbox under my arm, I climbed
in the frozen capsule and waited for you
to clear morning like the path through snow:
hot water on the windshield. Ten below.

We skidded past our milkman, late with deliveries.
The paperboy's bright hand catapulted goodbye.
In your Scottish complexion, I recognized mine,
pink, freckled. Its color dissolved

in the heater's breath. That morning, the scarf
at your neck wound a jet stream like Lindbergh's in Paris,
but the brim of your cap was embroidered with oak leaves,
and stitched on the back, the words *Tonkin Gulf*.

When we reached the schoolyard, I told you to take
care, my habit in leave-taking, as if care
were portable or compact like a parachute.
Your car veered toward the airfield and disappeared.

Those facts I have no use for. Twenty years
I dream your death-plane back, down the foggy night,
over the carrier, to the landing deck and hookmen's wire.
You kill the engine. Opening the cockpit,

your hand raises a sign of hello. I keep this picture
for every mission you flew. You are always climbing out
of your plane, its wing flaps down, cool, hangar-bound,
to show me a way, if not around, then through.

The Air Pilot's Wife

By March we've had our share of rain.
What's the point of living in the South
if you can't count on the weather?
With Easter only a week away,
the azaleas have taken their cue,
and the rosebushes will soon be
a horseshoe of color. I still prefer
yellow ones, though neighbors exclaim
over the new-dawn pink.
Of course, I'll give them some.
Yesterday, a deer and her fawn
came to the edge of the back lot.
They were so attentive to each other,
they didn't notice me.
Their cinnamon bodies were soft
and sleek in the afternoon
sun filtering through the pines.
They are Roman pines, I've discovered.
For a moment, with the light streaming down,
I thought I was in a cathedral.
There was no place to look but up.
When the deer bounded off, it was without
a sound, without disturbing a single
needle or cone. And there are plenty.
I often think of doing something
with the land out back, cultivating it
or building a guest-house,
but it's more nature's than mine.
I like the furrowing moles.

The destructive squirrels and loudmouthed
jays are here. They have their homes,
their mates. They go about their business,
which gives me pleasure.
I have this feeling for the land
which you had for the air,
or perhaps you had a feeling for the land
but from a different perspective.
You saw it day after day
and by night from a great distance.
How small the earth was to you.
I see things close-up.
I would get down on my hands and knees
to glimpse the first hint of iris.
With March arrived, there's all this
quickening. Sometimes,
I just want to talk with you.

The Pilot's Daughter

In the twilight I am fishing
from the train trestle
with a friend and my father,
our lines trailing the Chesapeake.
We have stood a good hour
and caught nothing,
until I pull from the depths
a black eel,
whose slithery, hard body
thumps and will not lie flat.

He is three feet long
with gun-metal eyes.
He coils and snaps. So I fall back,
while my friend, with a fast hand,
unhinges the torn mouth
and hacks him in two.
For her, my father has praise.

Walking home in the dark,
I relive the evening.
When I lie down at night,
the eel thrashes above my head.
I take him between my hands
for a brilliant electrocution.
We rise, leaving my father
utterly amazed.
I thought I would do anything
to please him.

If he returned from the deep
Pacific, if he towered over me
in his military whites
demanding courage,
I would say I face what I can,
hauling up this part of me
to examine closely,
circling and circling,

until I free it to the cold, gray bay.

Mission in Hong Kong

I looked for you
in the harbor's blue water.
I looked to see
if a carrier was in.
I looked for you
in the neon signs;
perhaps they were here then.

I went to the Star Ferry.
I walked in Victoria Park.
Did I see what you saw:
people taking their caged finches
for air? I traveled by tram
to Victoria Peak, spotted
the Hong Kong Hilton

where you stayed—
I went there.
I went to some bars.
I looked for you
in Kowloon and found
replicas of the gifts
you bought: porcelain cats,

a carved water buffalo.
I ate in a restaurant
you might have known.
I looked for you in the faces
of men on leave. I looked
for you in the streets
whose names I could not read.

My husband said to meet him
at Maiwo Yang, a tailor
who had made him a suit.
Maiwo Yang—the tag sewn
in your white shirt I wore
until I wore it away.
I ran as fast as I could.

I tried to note everything:
the weather, the hour, the steps
to the door, emblazoned with
Woolen Merchants & Tailors.
"Where is Mr. Maiwo Yang?" I asked.
Behind the racks of suits I found him.
"My father was here in 1966."

He smiled vaguely—my story
nothing new—and then,
with pins between his teeth,
resumed altering a trouser cuff,
bolts of nautical blue
adrift at his feet, from which
he might have cut a uniform for you.

Parade Ground

The black and white days are gone.
The green parade ground is blank
where midshipmen marched like wind-up toys,
their caps shellacked and bright as sails.
The flagpole knocks. A loose canopy

flaps over the empty reviewing stands.
Decorous wives of the captains have left.
The chairs are folded and kindling-stacked.
Only the monuments can endure the weather:
Tecumseh the chief, the iron anchor,

and the tomb with the body of John Paul Jones.
The black and white are gone like headlines.
Tears for "America" and the "Navy Hymn"
are packed in a cruise box under a flight jacket
with the days of right and the days of wrong.

The Severn idles near the parade ground.
The cherry and apple trees have started to bloom
along the road that runs to the cemetery,
then up the hill to the house where we lived
and looked out over a country turning thankless.

Stopping at the True, the Good, the Beautiful Company in Bac Ninh

After a cruise on the *Halong Dream,*
the guide informs us we will stop
at a typical silk and embroidery store,
only not exactly typical, since

its employees are orphans and children,
maimed by war after their mothers, exposed
to Agent Orange, bore them. Here,
they live and work, relatively secure.

Young and not-so-young are bent
over whirring machines and finished cloth
that they slowly embellish by hand.
I veer into the finished-products aisle—

dressing gowns, *ao dai*, table linens—
searching for something inexpensive,
lightweight, easy to pack,
like finger towels, which a British lady

says she had hoped to find because
they make the perfect house gift.
I agree. The manager following us
has no frame of reference, suggesting

a laundry-bag—three different sizes.
I choose a little one with drawstrings,
imagining what I could put inside:
some potpourri, bangles, tea?

Or perhaps regret, longing, and guilt.
I buy a dozen, each with a scene
of Vietnam carefully stitched
in thread so fine the eyes could dim

putting it there: a woman wearing
her conical hat with her buffalo
in a field of rice, which my father saw
and knew, high and small, from the air.

At the War Remnants Museum, Saigon

I will not look at the bomb
used for attacking motor vehicles or trains,
how it cuts animals and people
with six razors opening
like a turning helicopter blade.

I will not look at the large striated explosives
or the small, smooth orange one
that resembles a football,
with its muzzle velocity
of 1200 meters per second.

I will not stand long
in front of the napalm victims,
their hands wrapped like cocoons,
bodies marred beyond reconstruction,
the baby whose skin is gone.

I will not gaze at the XM41E2
gravel mine, dropped by AD-6 planes
over roads, populous towns,
and densely wooded areas,
the mines still buried in the land.

Ruined villages, temples, homes—
I will certainly not look at
the children touched by Agent Orange,
the malformed head floating
in an airtight jar. I will not look

at the rocket launcher,
containers of chemicals being prepared
for Operation Ranch Hand
out of Da Nang, all toxins
while U.S. and ARVN soldiers wear masks.

Defoliants, little dress burned,
a child's sandal, a woman's face
with a gun to her head at the Massacre of Huong Dien,
the girl imploring troops,
Don't kill my father.

Do not tarry here in history's dark rooms
when all that is behind us
and the sun is bursting outside
where Hung, our driver, who says he was
a VC guerrilla, smokes in the shade.

Water Buffalo

He lies cooling in mud, his head just visible.
My father bought his carved likeness years ago.
Chihuahua size, he stood on our living-room chest,
massive horns swept up in a lethal headdress,
or so I thought, his eyes large and sad. I want
my picture taken, so I squat by the water,

nervously smiling, asking my husband to hurry,
click the shutter. Before he can, the buffalo
stirs to climb the bank, which I hear and leap back,
making the Vietnamese gathered around laugh:
He won't hurt you. He only wants to smell your skin
which is new to him. Poor buffalo, gentle,

misunderstood, my alarm sends him reeling.
I extend my arm and hold myself rock still
as he rumbles out once more, all grey one ton,
snorting and breathing me in without censure
or grudge, his breath an unexpected answer to
my ignorance, his hide, tough velvet like forgiveness.

My Father Meets Amelia Earhart

After my father's plane crashed in the Pacific,
I used to think how sad that he was
alone when he died, strapped
in his fighter jet, latitude and longitude
unknown, his recovery barred,

no one to bear his casket to the family plot.
Yet now I imagine Amelia with Noonan
in tow, on hand to greet him.
After twenty-nine years in a similar fix,
she welcomed a traveler who shared her passion.

He would have liked her, of course,
and she him, both being thirty-nine, handsome,
death-wed too early, like Icarus.
They could talk shop—his Skyhawk
versus her Electra, compare hops and their DFCs,

play rummy. In time they would grow
philosophical over how events played out,
how a lack of choice brought them there
(tragedy's common element) or so they thought—
she with her compulsion to follow through

despite the signs of a doomed endeavor
and he with his outsize sense of duty
to lead his squadron back to the Tonkin Gulf.
His father, the admiral with Pentagon ties,
could have pulled strings, and G.P. counseled

Amelia in Lae to stop. But no,
locked into circumstances, they cradled
their fates. And still, they look on the bright side:
neither suffered the indignities of old age;
both became legends in people's minds.

He would have been pleased to idle
with this pioneer of aviation who chirped
Violet and *Cheerio* on take-off,
the first woman to lecture the middies at Annapolis.
If he sent me a postcard, it might say:

Your grandfather may have posed
for a photograph with Will Rogers
on the flight deck,
but I'm spending Eternity
with the Queen of the Air.

Ornaments in August

High on a shelf in the top hall closet,
stashed there ten years ago after she died,
are Mother's tree ornaments,
dozens of glass-blown globes:
blue, silver, gold—swaddled in tissue,
well organized in a box stamped
"The Dolly Tot Company."
The box must have brought
a toy to my brother or me, but what?
And which Christmas exactly—before
or after our father died, two weeks shy
of their sixteenth anniversary in December?

The effusive "brite lights," cradled like eggs,
the tarnish-proof tinsel garlands
(flame-proof, "as advertised in *Life*":
18 feet for 59 cents) don't square
with what I recall she felt about Christmas.
By nine p.m., she collapsed in tears:
It was all too much. But mostly she kept
her emotions tightly wrapped,
producing the holiday each year as if
nothing were wrong, being bound
to a forced march. Here she kept
two snowy spheres, signed with
a glittery salutation: *Merry Xmas from
Lacey and Bob Eckhart*—who were they?

Now I think,
here's how to move on: gather
the ornaments—those that are good—
to ship to my brother (one bears his name,
in our father's hand); mark the package:
Open in August. Then toss
the tinsel that won't ever tarnish,
glass necklaces with their missing beads;
release the clip bird with its rusted spring,
whose ragged feathers bespeak a storm
of years, trapped in a sealed box
behind the painted-shut cabinet doors.

Veterans Day

in memory of my father (1927—1966)

I forgive you for dying. Forty-five years after
the fact, I forgive the carrier captain who ordered
your flight in the rain and fog. I forgive the plane,
if the controls locked, preventing you from pulling up.
I forgive the starless night, the horizon you could not see.
I forgive the waves that swallowed you.
I forgive the catapult and flight-deck crew,
who inspected the plane, then waved you off.
I forgive your father, the admiral, who would not intervene.
I forgive the president, who sent you to war twice.
I forgive the air, your last breath, the reason I'll never know
you could not eject. I forgive the officials
who came to our house with the news that you were missing
and the disc jockey who broadcast your loss.
I forgive my schoolmates, whose fathers went on living,
and the friends who wore black armbands.
I forgive the ideas you died for: duty, country, honor.
I forgive you for being young, for needing your father's approval.
I forgive myself for judging you,
since you could never speak or explain.
I forgive my anger and grief, still quick, my wanting you back—
a child, still, as I live my life without you.

Leonidas at Thermopylae

A warrior must not be in love with life.
To conquer or die has always been our law.
What I have done was all for Sparta's fame.
We held the wall; we pushed the Persians back,

but our two-day battle has come to this:
bodies and blood, while a messenger reports
the enemy takes a goat path through the leaves
to decimate our flank, or what remains.

I've let the men disperse—why should they stay
when defeat is guaranteed? Curse the traitor
who shared our evening food, our fire and tent,
dissembling every day, eager to whisper

in Xerxes' ear a mountain route around
the pass we block and so outnumber us—
ten thousand to one. I do not fault the men
for going. See, they flee like startled birds.

And still a phalanx stands, fully armed
with sword and shield, awaiting my command.
What brave or foolish men they are,
my own three hundred. I selected each one

by hand for valor, loyalty, and strength,
not dwelling on the chance of death,
but certain that if death came it would be good.
Who in the final instant judges it so?

They have trained for this since they were boys.
Yet don't they have a home, a beloved's arms,
the dream of another spring in the Peloponnese?
Although I am a Spartan and their king,

I long to witness my daughter's wedding feast,
the unborn children of my son, my wife's
black hair as it begins to silver. Oh,
the olive tree and poppies beside our door—

How weary I am. How hard to bear my part,
as though, like Atlas, I carry the world and more:
an awareness of our fate within the hour,
sharper than any arrow, sting, or blow.

I see my own blood flowing toward the sea,
the Persian who will cut me down like grass.
When I was young, I never imagined this day,
and yet my men are waiting. They attend my words.

What can I tell them they don't already know?
We die because we are soldiers—that is our job.
In seeing it through to the end, we most excel
and like a crashing wave become ourselves.

Here, at the Gates of Fire, our deaths will serve
as an altar and our doom will lead to praise:
They fought with spear and sword, hands and teeth;
in dying they granted their citizens time to rally.

My wife, my love, dearer to me than life,
our union has been long and pure, finer
than most. I think of the tender olive wreath
interlaced with roses that you made.

I've tied a lock of your hair behind my shield,
where I place my hand. How lucky I am
to have the story I leave: I died with honor,
your name on my lips and the city in which you live.

Men, come let us oil our bodies to gleam
and pour a libation out to arriving dawn.
Shoulder to shoulder make our circle stand
that poets sing about us when we are gone.

Blue Raft
for my daughter

The first month you floated in me
at the beach of my childhood,
the sun burned my shoulders.
Black crows appeared
among the sandpipers and gulls.
The crows were the only darkness,
out of place with their splayed crow feet,
unable to run or dive like sea-birds.
I watched them on the shore,
donax in their sharp beaks.
I couldn't say whether theirs
was a taste born of necessity or desire.
One looked at me with its hard, berry eyes,
and I looked back,
each of us suspecting the other.
Then I took the blue raft
from summers before and went out
beyond the waves to flutter-kick and drift.
The ocean was smooth as a platter,
strewn with stars.
I wanted to drift for hours
in forgetful peace,
right into oblivion,
with only the ocean to buoy me
and no one in the houses to call me.
The houses seemed very small
and far away.
When I drifted close to the shrimpers,
a shrill whistle woke me.
I was out too far.
I started to paddle and kick.
All the while I thought of you
floating inside me—
out too far, out too far.

At last I reached the point
where waves swell,
and a wave lifted the raft
high, then down.
The foam enveloped me
the way it would when I'd ride
on my father's back,
a knapsack, a small burden
among salty pleasure.
I skidded over the broken shells
to ankle-deep water, and as I rose,
taking the blue raft lightly under my arm,
salt and sand clinging to me,
I thought of how my father would say,
lying on a raft in the Atlantic,
This is the life. He was dead,
but you were floating in me,
and the crows, like some new part
of myself, stood on the beach,
exquisitely black, shining.

Born in Florida into a military family, **Gardner McFall** is the author of two books of poems, two children's books, and an opera libretto entitled *Amelia* (University of Washington Press), inspired by her Navy pilot father's life and death in the Vietnam War. Her poems have appeared in *The Atlantic Monthly, The New Republic, Southwest Review, The Sewanee Review, The New Yorker, The Nation, Poet Lore,* and *The Hopkins Review.* She is also the editor of *Made with Words: A Prose Miscellany* by May Swenson (University of Michigan Press) and wrote the introduction and notes for a Barnes and Noble Classics edition of Kenneth Grahame's *The Wind in the Willows.*

She received a B.A. from Wheaton College in Massachusetts, an M.A. in the Writing Seminars from The Johns Hopkins University, and a Ph.D. from New York University. She has taught at Hunter College and The Cooper Union. The recipient of a Discovery/ *The Nation* award, *The Missouri Review*'s Thomas McAfee Prize for Poetry, and residencies from Yaddo, the MacDowell Colony, and the Virginia Center for the Creative Arts, she lives and works in New York. This chapbook is a collection of poems about her father's military service, his death, and their consequences.